I0163097

The Search After Happiness by Hannah More

A Pastoral Drama

'To rear the tender thought,
To teach the young idea how to shoot,
To pour the fresh instruction o'er the mind,
To breathe th' enlivening spirit, and to fix
The generous purpose in the female breast.'
Thomson.

Hannah More was born on February 2nd, 1745 at Fishponds in the parish of Stapleton, near Bristol. She was the fourth of five daughters.

The City of Bristol, at that time, was a centre for slave-trading and Hannah would, over time, become one of its staunchest critics.

She was keen to learn, possessed a sharp intellect and was assiduous in studying. Hannah first wrote in 1762 with The Search after Happiness (by the mid-1780s some 10,000 copies had been sold).

In 1767 Hannah became engaged to William Turner. After six years, with no wedding in sight, the engagement was broken off. Turner then bestowed upon her an annual annuity of £200. This was enough to meet her needs and set her free to pursue a literary career.

Her first play, The Inflexible Captive, was staged at Bath in 1775. The famous David Garrick himself produced her next play, Percy, in 1777 as well as writing both the Prologue and Epilogue for it. It was a great success when performed at Covent Garden in December of that year.

Hannah turned to religious writing with Sacred Dramas in 1782; it rapidly ran through nineteen editions. These and the poems Bas-Bleu and Florio (1786) mark her gradual transition to a more serious and considered view of life.

Hannah contributed much to the newly-founded Abolition Society including, in February 1788, her publication of Slavery, a Poem recognised as one of the most important of the abolition period.

Her work now became more evangelical. In the 1790s she wrote several Cheap Repository Tracts which covered moral, religious and political topics and were both for sale or distributed to literate poor people. The most famous is, perhaps, The Shepherd of Salisbury Plain, describing a family of incredible frugality and contentment. Two million copies of these were circulated, in one year.

In 1789, she purchased a small house at Cowslip Green in Somerset. She was instrumental in setting up twelve schools in the area by 1800.

She continued to oppose slavery throughout her life, but at the time of the Abolition Bill of 1807, her health did not permit her to take as active a role in the movement as she had done in the late 1780s, although she maintained a correspondence with Wilberforce and others.

In July 1833, the Bill to abolish slavery throughout the British Empire passed in the House of Commons, followed by the House of Lords on August 1st.

Hannah More died on September 7th, 1833.

Index of Contents

PERSONS OF THE DRAMA

Four young Ladies of distinction, in Search of Happiness:—
Euphelia,
Cleora,
Pastorella,
Laurinda,

Urania, an ancient Shepherdess.
Her daughters:—
Sylvia,
Eliza,
Florella, a young shepherdess.

TO MRS GWATKIN

Dear Madam,

As the following Poem turns chiefly on the danger of Delay or Error in the important article of Education, I know not to whom I can, with more propriety, dedicate it, than to you, as the subject it inculcates has been one of the principal objects of your attention in your own family.

Let not the name of Dedication alarm you; I am not going to offend you by making your Eulogium. Panegyric is only necessary to suspicious characters; Virtue will not accept it; Delicacy will not offer it.

The friendship with which you have honoured me from my childhood, will, I flatter myself, induce you to pardon me for venturing to lay before you this public testimony of my esteem, and to assure you how much I am,

Dear Madam,
Your obedient
And obliged humble servant,
THE AUTHOR.

PREFACE

The object of the following Poem, which was written in very early youth, was an earnest wish to furnish a substitute for the very improper custom, which then prevailed, of allowing plays, and those not always of the purest kind, to be acted by young Ladies in boarding schools. And it has afforded a serious satisfaction to the Author to learn that this little Poem, and likewise the Sacred Dramas, have very frequently been adopted to supply the place of those more dangerous amusements. If it may be still happily instrumental in promoting a regard to Religion and Virtue in the minds of young persons, and afford them an innocent, and perhaps not altogether unuseful, amusement in the exercise of recitation, the end for which it was originally composed, and the author's utmost wish in its re-publication, will be fully answered.

PROLOGUE

Spoken By A Young Lady.

In these grave scenes, and unembellish'd strains,
Where neither sly intrigue nor passion reigns;
How dare we hope an audience will approve
A Drama void of wit, and free from love?
Where no soft Juliet sighs, and weeps, and starts,
No fierce Roxana takes by storm your hearts;
No comic ridicule, no tragic swagger,
Not one elopement, not one bowl or dagger?
No husband wrong'd, who trusted and believed,
No father cheated, and no friend deceived;
No libertine in glowing strains described,
No lying chambermaid that rake had bribed:
Nor give we, to reward the rover's life,
The ample portion and the beauteous wife:
Behold, to raise the manners of the age,
The frequent moral of the scenic page!
And shall we then transplant these noxious scenes
To private life? to misses in their teens?
The pompous tone, the masculine attire,
The stilts, the buskin, the dramatic fire,

Corrupt the softness of the gentler kind,
And taint the sweetness of the youthful mind.
Ungovern'd passions, jealousy and rage,
But ill become our sex, still less our age;
Whether we learn too well what we describe,
Or fail the Poet's meaning to imbibe;
In either case your blame we justly raise,
In either lose, or ought to lose, your praise.
How dull, if tamely flows th' impassion'd strain;
If well — how bad to be the thing we feign;
To fix the mimic scene upon the heart,
And keep the passions when we quit the part!
Such are the perils the dramatic muse,
In youthful bosoms threatens to infuse;
Our timid Author labours to impart
A less pernicious lesson to the heart;
What, though no charm of melody divine,
Smooth her round period, or adorn her line;
Though her unpolish'd page in vain aspires
To emulate the graces she admires;
Though destitute of skill, her sole pretence
But aims at simple truth and common sense;
Yet shall her honest unassuming page
Tell that its Author in a modish age,
Preferr'd plain virtue to the boast of art,
Nor fix'd one dangerous maxim on the heart.
Oh if, to crown her efforts, she could find,
They rooted but one error from one mind;
If in the bosom of ingenuous youth
They stamp'd one useful thought, one lasting truth,
'Twould be a fairer tribute to her name,
Than loud applause, or an empty fame!

THE SEARCH AFTER HAPPINESS

SCENE — A Grove

EUPHELIA, CLEORA, PASTORELLA, LAURINDA

CLEORA
Welcome, ye humble vales, ye flow'ry shades,
Ye crystal fountains, and ye silent glades!
From the gay misery of the thoughtless great,
The walks of folly, the disease of state;
From scenes where daring guilt triumphant reigns,
Its dark suspicions and its hoard of pains;

Where Pleasure never comes without alloy,
And Art but thinly paints fallacious joy;
Where Languour loads the day, Excess the night,
And dull Satiety succeeds Delight;
Where midnight Vices their fell orgies keep,
And guilty Revels scare the phantom Sleep;
Where Dissipations wears the name of Bliss:
From these we fly in search of Happiness.

EUPHELIA
Not the tir'd Pilgrim, all his dangers past,
When he descries the long-sought shrine at last;
E'er felt a joy so pure as this fair field,
These peaceful shades, and smiling valleys yield;
For sure, these oaks, which old as Time appear,
Proclaim Urania's lonely dwelling near.

PASTORELLA
How the description with the scene agrees!
Here lowly thickets, there aspiring trees;
The hazel copse excluding noon-day's beam,
The tufted arbour, the pellucid stream;
The blooming sweet-briar, and the hawthorn shade,
The springing cowslips, and the daisy'd mead;
The wild luxuriance of the full-blown fields,
Which Spring prepares, and laughing Summer yields!

EUPHELIA
Here simple Nature strikes the enraptured eye
With charms, which wealth and art but ill supply;
The genuine graces, which without we find,
Display the beauty of the owner's mind.

LAURINDA
These deep embowering shades conceal the cell,
Where sage Urania and her daughters dwell:
Florella too, if right we've heard the tale,
With them resides — the lilly of the vale.

CLEORA
But soft; what gentle female form appears,
Which smiles of more than mortal beauty wears?
Is it the Guardian Genius of the grove?
Or some fair angel from the choirs above!

[Enter **FLORELLA**, who speaks.

Whom do I see? ye beauteous virgins, say,

What chance conducts your steps this lonely way?
Do you pursue some favourite lambkin stray'd?
Or do yon alders court you to their shade?
Declare, fair strangers! If aright I deem,
No rustic nymph of vulgar rank you seem.

CLEORA

No cooling shades allure our eager sight,
Nor lambkins lost, our searching steps invite.

FLORELLA

Or is it, haply, yonder branching vine,
Whose tendrils round our low-roof'd cottage twine;
Whose spreading height, with purple clusters crown'd,
Attracts the gaze of every nymph around?
Have these lone regions aught that charms beside?
Yours are my shades, my flowers, my fleecy pride.

EUPHELIA

Florella! our united thanks receive;
Sole proof of gratitude we have to give:
And since you deign to ask, O courteous fair!
The motive of our unremitting care;
Know then, kind maid, our joint researches tend
To find that sovereign good of life, a friend;
From whom the wholesome counsel we may gain,
How our young hearts may happiness obtain.
By Fancy's mimic pencil oft portray'd,
Still have we woo'd the visionary maid:
The lovely phantom mocks our eager eyes;
And still we chase, and still we miss the prize!

CLEORA

Long have we search'd throughout this bounteous isle,
With constant ardour and with ceaseless toil;
The various ways of various life we've tried;
But still the bliss we seek has been deny'd.
We've sought in vain through every different state;
The murmuring poor, the discontented great.
If Peace, and Joy, in palaces reside,
Or in obscurer haunts delight to hide;
If Happiness with worldly pleasures dwell,
Or shrouds her graces in the hermit's cell:
If Wit, if Science, teach the road to bliss,
Or torpid dulness find the joys they miss;
To learn this truth, we've bid a long adieu
To all the shadows blinded men pursue.
— We seek Urania; whose sagacious mind

May lead our steps this latent good to find:
Her worth we emulate; her virtues fire
Our ardent hearts to be what we admire:
For though with care she shuns the public eye,
Yet worth like hers, unknown can never lie.

LAURINDA
On such a fair faultless model form'd,
By Prudence guided, and by Virtue warm'd,
Perhaps Florella can direct our youth,
And point our footsteps to the paths of Truth.

FLORELLA
Ill would it suit my unexperienced age
In such important questions to engage.
Young as I am, unskilful to discern,
Nor fit to teach, who yet have much to learn.
But would you with maturer years advise,
And reap the counsel of the truly wise,
The dame in whom such worth and wisdom meet,
All that the world calls great she once possess'd,
With wealth, with rank, her prosperous youth was bless'd.
In adverse fortune, now, serene and gay,
'Who gave,' she said, 'had right to take away.'
Two lovely daughters bless her growing years,
And, by their virtues, well repay her cares.
With them, beneath her sheltering wing I live,
And share the bounties she has still to give;
For Heaven, who in its dispensations join'd
A narrow fortune to a noble mind,
Has bless'd the sage Urania with a heart
Which Wisdom's noblest treasures can impart;
In Duty's active roud each day is past,
As if she thought each day might prove her last:
Her labours for devotion best prepare,
And meek Devotion smooths the brow of Care.

PASTORELLA
Then lead, Florella, to that humble shed
Where Peace resides: from courts and cities fled;

SONG
O Happiness, celestial fair,
Our earliest hope, our latest care,
Oh hear our fond request!
Vouchsafe, reluctant Nymph, to tell
On what sweet spot thou lov'st to dwell,
And make us truly blest.

Amidst the walks of public life,
The toils of wealth, ambition's strife,
We long have sought in vain:
The crowded city's noisy din,
And all the busy haunts of men,
Afford but care and pain.

Pleased with the soft, the soothing power
Of calm Reflection's silent hour,
Sequester'd dost thou dwell?
Where care and tumult ne'er intrude,
Dost thou reside with Solitude?
Thy humble votaries tell.

O Happiness, celestial fair,
Our earliest hope, our latest care
Let us not sue in vain!
O deign to hear our fond request,
Come, take possession of our breast,
And there for ever reign.

SCENE — The Grove

URANIA, SYLVIA, ELIZA

SYLVIA (singing).
Sweet Solitude, thou placid queen
Of modest air, and brow serene!
'Tis thou inspirest the Sage's themes;
The poet's visionary dreams.

Parent of Virtue, nurse of Thought!
By thee were Saints and Patriarchs taught;
Wisdom from thee her treasures drew,
And in thy lap fair Science grew.

Whate'er exalts, refines, and charms,
Invites to thought, to virtue warms;
Whate'er is perfect, fair, and good,
We owe to thee, sweet Solitude!

In these blest shades, O still maintain
Thy peaceful, unmolested reign!
Let no disorder'd thoughts intrude
On thy repose, sweet Solitude!

With thee the charm of life shall last,
Although its rosy bloom be past;
Shall still endure when Time shall spread
His silver blossoms o'er my head.

No more with this vain world perplex'd,
Thou shalt prepare me for the next;
The springs of life shall gently cease,
And angels point the way to peace.

URANIA
Ye tender objects of maternal love,
Ye dearest joys my widow'd heart can prove,
Come, taste the glories of the new-born day,
And grateful homage to its author pay!
Oh! ever may this animating sight
Convey instruction while it sheds delight!
Does not that sun, whose cheering beams impart
Joy's glad emotions to the pure in heart;
Does not that vivid power teach every mind
To be as warm, benevolent and kind;
To burn with unremitted ardour still,
Like him to execute their Maker's will;
Then let us, Power Supreme! thy will adore.
Invoke thy mercies, and proclaim thy power.
Shalt thou these benefits in vain bestow?
Shall we forget the fountain whence they flow?
Teach us through these to lift our hearts to Thee,
And in the gift the bounteous giver see.
To view Thee as thou art, all good and wise,
Nor let thy blessings hide thee from our eyes.
From all obstructions clear our mental sight;
Pour on our souls thy beatific light!
Teach us thy wondrous goodness to revere,
With love to worship, and with reverence fear!
In the mild works of thy benignant hand,
As in the thunder of thy dread command.
In common objects we neglect thy power,
While wonders shine in every plant and flower.
— Tell me, my first, my last, my darling care,
If you this morn have raised your hearts in prayer?
Say, did you rise from the sweet bed of rest,
Your God unpraised, his holy name unblest?

SYLVIA
Our hearts with gratitude and rev'rence fraught,
By those pure precepts you have ever taught;

By your example, more than precept strong,
Of pray'r and praise have tun'd their matin song.

ELIZA
With ever-new delight, we now attend
The counsels of our fond maternal friend.

[Enter **FLORELLA**, with **EUPHELIA, CLEORA, PASTORELLA, LAURINDA**.

FLORELLA (Aside to the Ladies).
See how the goodly dame, with pious art,
Makes each event a lesson to the heart!
Observe the duteous list'ners how they stand!
Improvement and delight go hand in hand.

URANIA
But where's Florella?

FLORELLA
Here's the happy she,
Whom Heaven most favor'd when it gave her thee.

URANIA
But who are these, in whose attractive mien,
So sweetly blended, ev'ry grace is seen?
Speak, my Florella! say the cause why here
These beauteous damsels on our plains appear?

FLORELLA
Invited hither by Urania's fame,
To seek her friendship, to these shades they came.
Straying alone at morning's earliest dawn,
I met them wand'ring on the distant lawn.
Their courteous manners soon engag'd my love:
I've brought them here your sage advice to prove.

URANIA
Tell me, ye gentle nymphs, the reason tell,
Which brings such guests to grace my lowly cell?
My pow'r of serving, tho' indeed but small,
Such as it is, you may command it all.

CLEORA
Your counsel, your advice, is all we ask!
And for Urania that's no irksome task.
'Tis happiness we seek: O deign to tell
Where the coy fugitive delights to dwell!

URANIA

Ah, rather say where you have sought this guest,
This lovely inmate of the virtuous breast?
Declare the various methods you've essay'd
To court and win the bright celestial maid.
But first, tho' harsh the task, each beauteous fair
Her ruling passion must with truth declare.
From evil habits own'd, from faults confess'd,
Alone we trace the secrets of the breast.

EUPHELIA

Bred in the regal splendours of a court,
Wher pleasures, dress'd in every shape, resort,
I try'd the pow'r of pomp and costly glare,
Nor e'er found room for thought, or time for pray'r:
In diff'rent follies ev'ry hour I spent;
I shunn'd Reflection, yet I sought Content.
My hours were shar'd betwixt the park and play,
And music serv'd to waste the tedious day;
Yet softest airs no more with joy I heard,
If any sweeter warbler was preferr'd;
The dance succeeded, and, succeeding, tir'd,
If some more graceful dancer were admir'd.
No sounds but flatt'ry ever sooth'd my ear:
Ungentle truths I knew not how to bear.
The anxious day induc'd the sleepless night,
And my vex'd spirit never knew delight;
Coy Pleasure mock'd me with delusive charms;
Still the thin shadow fled my clasping arms.
Or if some actual joy I seem'd to taste,
Another's pleasures laid my blessings waste:
One truth I prov'd, that lurking Envy hides
In ev'ry heart where Vanity presides.
A fairer face would rob my soul of rest,
And fix a scorpion in my wounded breast.
Or, if my elegance of form prevail'd,
And haply her inferior graces fail'd;
Yet still some cause of wretchedness I found,
Some barbed shaft my shatter'd peace to wound.
Perhaps her gay attire exceeded mine—
When she was finer, how could I be fine?

SYLVIA

Pardon my interruption, beauteous maid!
Can Truth have prompted what you just have said?
What! can the poor pre-eminence of dress
Ease the pain'd heart, or give it happiness?
Or can you think your robes, tho' rich and fine,

Possess intrinsic value more than mine?

URANIA
So close our nature is to vice ally'd,
Our very comforts are the source of pride;
And dress, so much corruptio reigns within,
Is both the consequence and cause of sin.

CLEORA
Of Happiness unfound I too complain,
Sought in a diff'rent path, but sought in vain!
I sigh'd for fame, I languish'd for renown,
I would be flatter'd, prais'd, admir'd, and known.
On daring wing my mounting spirit soar'd,
And Science through her boundless fields explored:
I scorn'd the salique laws of pedant schools,
Which chain our genius down by tasteless rules:
I long'd to burst these female bonds, which held
My sex in awe, by vanity impell'd:
To boast each various faculty of mind,
Thy graces, Pope! with Johnson's learning join'd:
Like Swift, with strongly pointed ridicule,
To brand the villain, and abash the fool:
To judge with taste, with spirit to compose,
Now mount in epic, now descend to prose;
To join, like Burke, the Beauteous and Sublime,
Or build, with Milton's art, 'the lofty rhyme;'
Thro' Fancy's fields I rang'd ; I strove to hit
Melmoth's chaste style, and Prior's easy wit:
Thy classic graces, Mason, to display,
And court the Muse of Elegy with Gray:
I rav'd of Shakespeare's flame and Dryden's rage,
And ev'ry charm of Otway's melting page.
I talk'd by rote the jargon of the schools,
Of critic laws, and Artistotle's rules!
Of passion, sentiment, and style, and grace,
And unities of action, time, and place.
The daily duties of my life forgot,
To study fiction, incident, and plot:
Howe'er the conduct of my life might err,
Still my dramatic plans were regular.

URANIA
Who aims at ev'ry science, soon will find
The field how vast, how limited the mind!

CLEORA
Abstruser studies soon my fancy caught,

The poet in th' astronomer forgot:
The schoolmen's systems now my mind employ'd,
Their crystal Spheres, their Atoms, and their Void,
Newton and Halley all my soul inspir'd,
And numbers less than calculations fir'd;
Descartes, and Euclid, shar'd my varying breast,
And plans and problems all my soul possess'd.
Less pleas'd to sing inspiring Phoebus' ray,
Than mark the flaming comet's devious way.
The pale moon dancing on the silver stream,
And the mild lustre of her trembling beam,
No more could charm my philosophic pride,
Which sought her influence on the flowing tide.
No more ideal beauties fix'd my thought,
Which only facts and demonstrations sought.
Let common eyes, I said, with transport view
The earth's bright verdure, or the heaven's soft blue,
False is the pleasure; the delight is vain,
Colours exist but in the vulgar brain.
I now with Locke trod metaphysic soil,
Now chas'd coy Nature thro' the tracts of Boyle;
To win the wreath of Fame, by Science twin'd,
More than the love of Science fir'd my mind.
I seized on Learning's superficial part,
And title-page and index got by heart;
Some learn'd authority I still would bring
To grace my talk, and prove — the plainest thing:
This the chief transport I from science drew,
That all might know how much Cleora knew.
Not love, but wonder I aspir'd to raise,
And miss'd affection, while I grasp'd at praise.

PASTORELLA
To me, no joys could pomp or fame impart;
Far softer thoughts possess'd my virgin heart.
No prudent parent form'd my ductile youth,
Nor lead my footsteps in the paths of truth.
Left to myself to cultivate my mind,
Pernicious novels their soft entrance find:
Their pois'nous influence led my mind astray:
I sigh'd for something,— what,— I could not say.
I fancy'd virtues which were never seen,
And died for heroes who have never been;
I sicken'd with disgust at sober sense,
And loath's the pleasures worth and truth dispense:
I scorn'd the manners of the world I saw;
My guide was fiction, and romance my law.
Distemper'd thoughts my wand'ring fancy fill,

Each wind a zephyr, and each brook a rill;
I found adventures in each common tale,
And talk'd and sigh'd to every passing gale;
Convers'd with echoes, woods, and shades, and bowers,
Cascades, and grottos, fields, and streams, and flowers.
Retirement, more than crowds, had learn'd to please;
For treach'rous Leisure feeds the soft disease.
There, plastic Fancy ever moulds at will
Th' obedient image with a dang'rous skill;
The charming fiction, with alluring art,
Awakes the passions, and infects the heart.
A fancy'd heroine, an ideal wife;
I loath'd the offices of real life.
These all were dull and tame, I long'd to prove
The gen'rous ardours of unequal love;
Some marvel still my wayward heart must strike,
Or prince, or peasant, each had charms alike:
Whate'er inverted nature, custom, law,
With joy I courted, and with transport saw.
In the dull walk of Virtue's quiet round,
No aliment my fever'd fancy found,
Each duty to perform observant still
But those which God and Nature bade me fill.

ELIZA (to **URANIA**.)
O save me from the errors of deceit,
And all the dangers wealth and beauty meet.

PASTORELLA
Reason perverted, Fancy on her throne,
My soul to all my sex's softness prone;
I neither spoke nor look'd as mortal ought;
To sense abandon'd and by Folly taught:
A victim to Imagination's sway,
Which stole my health, and rest, and peace away:
Professions, void of meaning, I receiv'd,
And still I found them false — and still believ'd:
Imagin'd all who courted me approv'd;
Who prais'd, esteem'd me; and who flatter'd lov'd.
Fondly I hop'd, (now vain those hopes appear,)
Each man was faithful, and each maid sincere.
Still Disappointment mock'd the ling'ring day;
Still new-born wishes led my soul astray.
When in the rolling year no joy I find,
I trust the next; the next will sure be kind.
The next, fallacious as the last appears,
And sends me on to still remoter years.
They come, they promise — but forget to give;

I live not, but I still intend to live.
At length, deceiv'd in all my schemes of bliss,
I join'd these three in search of Happiness.

ELIZA

Is this the world of which we want a sight?
Are these the beings who are call'd polite?

SYLVIA

If so, O gracious Heaven! hear Sylvia's prayer:
Preserve me still in humble virtue here!
Far from such baneful pleasures may I live,
And keep, O keep, me from the taint they give!

LAURINDA

No love of Fame my torpid bosom warms,
No Fancy soothes me, and no Pleasure charms!
Yet still remote from Happiness I stray,
No guiding star illumes my trackless way.
My mind, nor wit misleads, nor passion goads,
But the dire rust of indolence corrodes;
This eating canker, with malignant stealth,
Destroys the vital powers of moral health.
Till now, I've slept on Life's tumultuous tide,
No principle of action for my guide.
From Ignorance my chief misfortunes flow;
I never wish'd to learn, or cared to know.
With every folly slow-paced time beguiled:
In size a woman, but in soul a child.
In slothful ease my moments crept away,
And busy trifles fill'd the tedious day;
I lived extempore, as Fancy fired,
As Chance directed, or Caprice inspired:
Too indolent to think, too weak to choose,
Too soft to blame, too gentle to refuse:
My character was stamp'd from those around;
The figures they, my mind the simple ground.
Fashion, with monstrous forms, the canvas stain'd,
Till nothing of my genuine self remain'd;
My pliant soul from Chance received its bent,
And neither good perform'd, or evil meant.
From right to wrong, from vice to virtue thrown,
No character possessing of its own.
To shun fatigue I made my only law;
Yet every night my wasted spirits saw.
No plan e'er mark'd the duties of the day,
Which stole in tasteless apathy away:
No energy inform'd my languid mind!

No joy the idle e'er must hope to find.
Weak indecision all my actions sway'd;
The day was lost before the choice was made.
Though more to folly than to guilt inclined,
A drear vacuity possess'd my mind.
Too old with infant sports to be amused,
Unfit for converse, and to books unused,
The wise avoided me, they could not hear
My senseless prattle with a patient ear.
I sought retreat, but found, with strange surprise,
Retreat is pleasant only to the wise;
The crowded world by vacant minds is sought,
Because it saves th' expense and pain of thought.
Disgusted, restless, every plan amiss,
I come with these in search of Happiness.

URANIA
O happy they for whom, in early age,
Enlightening knowledge spreads her letter'd page!
Teaches each headstrong passion to control,
And pours her liberal lesson on the soul!
Ideas grow from books, their natural food,
As aliment is changed to vital blood.
Though faithless Fortune strip her votary bare,
Though Malice haunt him, and though Envy tear,
Nor time, nor chance, nor want can e'er destroy
This soul-felt solace, and this bosom joy!

CLEORA
We thus united by one common fate,
Each discontented with her present state,
One common scheme pursue; resolved to know
If happiness can e'er be found below.

URANIA
Your candour, beauteous damsels, I approve,
Your foibles pity, and your merits love.
But ere I say the methods you must try
To gain the glorious prize for which you sigh,
Your fainting strength and spirits must be cheer'd
With a plain meal, by Temperance prepared.

FLORELLA
No luxury our humble board attends;
But Love and Concord are its smiling friends.

SONG
Hail, artless Simplicity, beautiful maid,

In the genuine attractions of Nature array'd;
Let the rich and the proud and the gay and the vain,
Still laugh at the graces that move in thy train.

No charm in thy modest allurements they find;
The pleasures they follow a sting leave behind.
Can criminal passion enrapture the breast
Like virtue, with peace and serenity blest?

Oh, would you Simplicity's precepts attend,
Like us, with delight at her altar you'd bend;
The pleasures she yields would with joy be embraced;
You'd practise from virtue, and love them from taste.

The linnet enchants us the bushes among,
Though cheap the musician, yet sweet is the song;
We catch the soft warbling in air as it floats,
And with ecstacy hang on the ravishing notes.

Our water is drawn from the clearest of springs,
And our food, nor disease nor satiety brings;
Our mornings are cheerful, our labours are blest
Our evenings are pleasant, our nights crown'd with rest.

From our culture yon garden its ornaments finds,
And we catch at the hint for improving our minds;
To live to some purpose we constantly try,
And we mark by our actions the days as they fly.

Since such are the joys that Simplicity yields,
We may well be content with our woods and our fields:
How useless to us, then, ye great, were your wealth,
When without it we purchase both pleasure and health!

[They retire into the Cottage.

SCENE. — A Rural Entertainment

FLORELLA, EUPHELIA, CLEORA, LAURINDA, PASTORELLA

FLORELLA (sings)
While Beauty and Pleasure are now in their prime,
And Folly and Fashion expect our whole time,
Ah! let not those phantoms our wishes engage:
Let us live so in youth, that we blush not in age.

Though the vain and the gay may allure us awhile,
Yet let not their flattery our prudence beguile:
Let us covet those charms that will never decay,
Nor listen to all that deceivers can say.

'How the tints of the rose, and the jasmine's perfume,
The eglantine's fragrance, the lilac's gay bloom,
Though fair and though fragrant, unheeded may lie,
For that neither is sweet when Florella is by.'

I sigh not for beauty, nor languish for wealth,
But grant me, kind Providence, virtue and health;
Then, richer than kings, and as happy as they
My days shall pass sweetly and swiftly away.

When age shall steal on me, and youth is no more,
And the moralist Time shakes his glass at my door,
What charm in lost beauty or wealth should I find
My treasure, my wealth, is a sweet peace of mind!

That peace I'll preserve then, as pure as was given,
And taste in my bosom an earnest of Heaven;
Thus Virtue and Wisdom can warm the cold scene,
And sixty may flourish as gay as sixteen.

And when long I the burthen of life shall have borne,
And Death with his sickle shall cut the ripe corn,
Resign'd to my fate, without murmur or sigh,
I'll bless the kind summons, and lie down and die.

EUPHELIA
Thus sweetly pass the hours of rural ease!
Here life is bliss, and pleasures truly please!

PASTORELLA
With joy we view the dangers we have past,
Assured we've found felicity at last.

FLORELLA
Esteem none happy by their outward air;
All have their portion of allotted care.
Though Wisdom wear the semblance of Content,
When the full heart with agony is rent,
Secludes its anguish from the public view,
And by secluding, learns to conquer too;
Denied the fond indulgence to complain,
The aching heart its peace may best regain.
By love directed, and in mercy meant,

Are trials suffer'd, and afflictions sent;
To stem impetuous Passion's furious tide,
To curb the insolence of prosperous Pride,
To wean from earth, and bid our wishes soar
Where weary'd Virtue shall for refuge fly,
And every tear be wiped from every eye.

CLEORA
Listening to you, my heart can never cease
To reverence Virtue, and to sigh for peace.

FLORELLA
Know, e'en Urania, that accomplish'd fair,
Whose goodness makes her Heaven's peculiar care,
Though born to all that affluence can bestow,
Has felt the deep reverse of human wo;
Yet meek in grief, and patient in distress,
She knew the hand that wounds has power to bless.
Grateful she bows, for what is left her still,
To Him whose love dispenses good and ill;
To Him who, while his bounty thousands fed,
Had not himself a place to lay his head;
To Him who, that he might our wealth insure,
Though rich himself, consented to be poor.
Taught by his precepts, by his practice taught
Her will submitted, and resigned her thought,
Through faith she looks beyond this dark abode,
To scenes of glory near the throne of God.

[Enter **URANIA, SYLVIA, ELIZA.**

URANIA
Since, gentle Nymphs, my friendship to obtain,
You've sought wth eager step this peaceful plain,
My honest counsel with attention hear,
Though plain, well meant; imperfect, yet sincere;
What from maturer years alone I've known,
What time has taught me and experience shown.
No polish'd phrase my artless speech will grace,
But unaffected candour fill its place:
My lips shall Flattery's smooth deceit refuse;
And truth be all the eloquence I'll use.
Know then, that life's chief happiness and wo,
From good or evil education flow;
And hence our future dispositions rise;
The vice we practise, or the good we prize.
When pliant nature any form receives,
That precept teaches or examples gives.

The yielding mind with virtue should be graced,
For first impressions seldom are effaced.
Then holy habits, then chastised desires,
Should regulate disorder'd Nature's fires.
If Ignorance then, her iron sway maintain,
If Prejudice preside, or Passion reign,
If Vanity preserve her native sway,
If selfish tempers cloud the opening day,
If no kind hand impetuous pride restrain,
But for the wholesome curb we give the rein;
The erring principle is rooted fast,
And fix'd the habit that through life may last.

PASTORELLA
With heartfelt penitence we now deplore
Those squander'd hours, which time can ne'er restore.

URANIA
Euphelia sighs for flattery, dress, and show;
Too common sources these of female wo!
In Beauty's sphere pre-eminence to find,
She slights the culture of th' immortal mind:
I would not rail at Beauty's charming power,
I would but have her aim at something more;
The fairest symmetry of form or face,
From intellect receives its highest grace;
The brightest eyes ne'er dart such piercing fires
As when a soul irradiates and inspires.
Beauty with reason needs not quite dispense,
And coral lips may sure speak common sense;
Beauty makes Virtue lovelier still appear:
Virtue makes Beauty more divinely fair!
Confirms its conquests o'er the willing mind,
And those your beauties gain, your virtues bind.
Yet would Ambition's fire your bosom fill,
Its flames repress not — be ambitious still;
Let nobler views your best attention claim,
The object changed, the engergy the same;
Those very passions which our heart invade,
If rightly pointed, blessings may be made.
Indulge the truth ambition to excel
In that best art — the art of living well.
But first extirpate from your youthful breast
That rankling torment which destroys your rest:
All other faults may take a higher aim,
But hopeless Envy must be still the same.
Some other passions may be turn'd to good,
But Envy must subdue, or be subdued.

This fatal gangrene to our moral life,
Rejects all palliatives, and asks the knife:
Excision spared, it tains the vital part,
And spreads its deadly venom to the heart.

EUPHELIA
Unhappy those to bliss who seek the way,
In power superior, or in splendour gay!
Inform'd by thee, no more vain man shall find
The charm of flattery taint Euphelia's mind:
By thee instructed, still my views shall rise,
Nor stop at any mark beneath the skies.

URANIA
In fair Laurinda's uninstructed mind,
The want of culture, not of sense, we find:
Whene'er you sought the good, or shunn'd the ill,
'Twas more from temper than from principle;
Your random life to no just rules reduced,
'Twas chance the virtue of the vice produced.
The casual goodness Impulse has to boast,
Like morning dews, or transient showers is lost
While Heaven-taught virtue pours her constant tide,
Like streams by living fountains still supplied.
Be wisdom still, though late, your earnest care,
Nor waste the precious hours in vain despair:
Associate with the good, attend the sage,
And meekly listen to experienced age.
What, if acquirements you have fail'd to gain
Such as the wise may want, the bad attain;
Yet still Religion's sacred treasures lie
Inviting, open, plain to every eye.
For every age, for every genius fit,
Nor limited to science nor to wit;
Not bound by taste, to genius not confined,
But all may learn the truths for all designed.
Though low the talents, and th' acquirements small,
The gift of grace divine is free to all;
She calls, solicits, courts you to be blest,
And points to mansions of eternal rest.
And when, advanced in years, matured in sense,
Think not with further care you may dispense;
'Tis fatal to the interests of the soul
To stop the race before we've reach'd the goal;
For nought our higher progress can preclude
So much as thinking we're already good.
The human heart ne'er knows a state of rest,
Bad leads to worse, and better tends to best.

We either gain or lose, we sink or rise,
Nor rests our struggling nature till she dies;
Then place the standard of Perfection high,
Pursue and grasp it, e'en beyond the sky.

LAURINDA

O that important Time could back return
Those mis-spent hours whose loss I deeply mourn
Accept, just Heaven, my penitence sincere,
My heartfelt anguish, and my fervant prayer!

URANIA

I pity Pastorella's hapless fate,
By nature gentle, generous, mild and great:
One false propension all her powers confined,
And chain'd her finer faculties of mind;
Yet every virtue might have flourish'd there
With early culture and maternal care.
If good we plant not, Vice will fill the place,
And rankest weeds the richest soils deface.
Learn, how ungovern'd thoughts the mind pervert,
And to disease all nourishment convert.
Ah! happy she, whose wisdom learns to find
A healthful fancy, and a well-train'd mind!
A sick man's wildest dreams less wild are found
Than the day-visions of a mind unsound.
Disorder'd phantasies indulged too much,
Like harpies, always taint whate'er they touch.
Fly soothing Solitude! fly vain Desire!
Fly such soft verse as fans the dangerous fire!
Seek action; 'tis the scene which virtue loves:
The vigorous sun not only shines, but moves.
From sickly thoughts with quick abhorrence start,
And rule the fancy if you'd rule the heart:
By active goodness, by laborious schemes,
Subdue wild visions, and delusive dreams.
No earthly good a Christian's views should bound,
For ever rising should his aims be found.
Leave that fictitious good your fancy feigns
For scenes where real bliss eternal reigns:
Look to that region of immortal joys,
Where fear disturbs not, nor possession cloys;
Beyond what Fancy forms of rosy bowers,
Or blooming chaplets of unfading flowers;
Fairer than e'er imagination drew,
Or poet's warmest visions ever knew.
Press eager onward to those blissful plains
Where life eternal, joy perpetual reigns.

PASTORELLA

I mourn the errors of my thoughtless youth,
And long, with thee, to tread the paths of truth.

URANIA

Learning is all the bright Cleora's aim;
She seeks the loftiest pinnacle of fame;
On interdicted ground presumes to stand,
And grasps at Science with a venturous hand;
The privilege of Man she dares invade,
And tears the chaplet from his laurel'd head.
Why found her merit on a foreign claim?
Why lose a substance to acquire a name?
Let the proud sex possess their vaunted powers;
Be other triumphs, other glories, ours!
The gentler charms which wait on female life,
Which grace the daughter and adorn the wife,
Be these our boast; yet these may well admit
Of various knowledge, and of blameless wit;
Of sense, resulting from a nurtured mind,
Of polish'd converse, and of taste refined:
Of that quick intuition of the best,
Which feels the graceful, and rejects the rest:
Which finds the right by shorter ways than rules:
An art which Nature teaches — not the schools.
Thus conquering Sevigne the heart obtains,
While Dacier only admiration gains.
Know, fair Aspirer, could you even hope
To speak like Stonehouse, or to write like Pope,
To all the wonders of the Poet's lyre,
Join all that taste can add, or wit inspire,
With every various power of learning fraught,
The flow of style and the sublime of thought;
Yet if the milder graces of the mind,
Graces peculiar to the sex design'd,
Good nature, patience, sweetness void of art;
If these embellish'd not your virgin heart,
You might be dazzling, but not truly bright;
Might glare, but not emit an useful light;
A meteor, not a star, you would appear;
For Woman shines but in her proper shpere.
Accomplishments by Heaven were sure designed,
Less to adorn than to amend the mind:
Each should contribute to this general end,
And all to virtue, as their centre, tend.
Th' acquirements, which our best esteem invite,
Should not project, but soften, mix, unite:

In glaring light not strongly be display'd,
But sweetly lost, and melted into shade.

CLEORA
Confused with shame, to thy reproofs I bend,
Thou best adviser, and thou truest friend!
From thee I'll learn to judge and act aright,
Humility with Knowledge to unite:
The finish'd character must both combine,
The perfect woman must in either shine.

URANIA
Florella shines adorn'd with every grace,
Her heart all virtue, as all charms her face:
Above the wretched, and below the great,
Kind Heaven has fix'd her in a middle state;
The demon Fashion never warp'd her soul,
Her passions move at Piety's control;
Her eyes the movements of her heart declare,
For what she dares to be, she dares appear;
Unlectured in Dissimulation's school,
To smile by precept, and to blush by rule,
Her thoughts ingenuous, ever open lie,
Nor shrink from close Inspection's keenest eye;
No dark disguise about her heart is thrown;
'Tis Virtue's interest fully to be known;
Her natural sweetness every heart obtains;
What Art and Affectation miss, she gains.
She smooths the path of my declining years,
Augments my comforts, and divides my cares.

PASTORELLA
O sacred Friendship! O exalted state!
The choicest bounty of indulgent fate!

URANIA
Let Woman then her real good discern,
And her true interests of Urania learn:
As some fair violet, loveliest of the glade,
Sheds its mild fragrance on the lonely shade,
Withdraws its modest head from public sight,
Nor courts the Sun, nor seeks the glare of light;
Should some rude hand profanely dare intrude,
And bear its beauties from its native wood,
Exposed abroad its languid colours fly,
Its form decays, and all its odours die;
So Woman born to dignify retreat,
Unknown to flourish, and unseen be great,

To give domestic life its sweetest charm,
With softness polish, and with virtue warm,
Fearful of Fame, unwilling to be known,
Should seek but Heaven's applauses and her own;
Hers be the task to seek the lonely cell
Where modest want and silent anguish dwell:
Raise the weak head, sustain the feeble knees,
Cheer the cold heart, and chase the dire disease.
The splendid deeds which only seek a name,
Are paid their just reward in present fame;
But know, the awful all-disclosing day,
The long arrear of secret worth shall pay;
Applauding Saints shall hear with fond regard,
And He, who witness'd here, shall there reward.

EUPHELIA
With added grace she pleads Religion's cause,
Who from her life her virtuous lesson draws.

URANIA
In vain, ye fair, from place to place you roam
For that true peace which must be found at home
Nor change of fortune, nor of scene can give
The bliss you seek, which in the soul must live.
Then look no more abroad; in your own breast
Seek the true seat of happiness and rest.
Nor small, my friends! the vigilance I ask;
Watch well yourselves, this is the Christian's task.
The cherish'd sin by each must be assail'd,
New efforts added, where the past have fail'd;
The darling error check'd, the will subdued,
The heart by penitence and pray'r renew'd.
Nor hope for perfect happiness below;
Celestial plants on earth reluctant grow:
He who our frail mortality did bear,
Though free from sin was not exempt from care.

CLEORA
Let's join to bless that Power who brought us here,
Adore his goodness, and his will revere;
Assured that Peace exists but in the mind,
And Piety alone that Peace can find.

URANIA
In its true light this transient life regard:
This is a state of trial, not reward.
Though rough the passage, peaceful is the port,
The bliss is perfect, the probation short.

Of human wit beware the fatal pride;
An useful follower, but a dangerous guide:
On holy Faith's aspiring pinions rise;
Assert your birth-right, and assume the skies.
Fountain of Being! teach us to devote
To Thee each purpose, action, word, and thought!
Thy grace our hope, thy love our only boast,
Be all distinction in the Christian lost!
Be this in every state our wish alone,
Almighty, Wise and Good, Thy will be done!

Hannah More - A Short Biography

Hannah More was born on February 2nd, 1745 at Fishponds in the parish of Stapleton, near Bristol. She was the fourth of five daughters of Jacob More, a schoolmaster. He was originally from a family of Presbyterians in Norfolk, but had become a member of the Church of England to pursue a career in the Church. After losing a lawsuit over an estate he had hoped to inherit, he moved to Bristol, becoming an excise officer and later a teacher at the Fishponds free school.

The City of Bristol, at that time, was a centre for slave-trading and Hannah would, over time, become one of its staunchest critics.

The More's were a close family and all the sisters were educated at first by their father who taught them Latin and mathematics. Hannah was also taught French by her elder sisters. Her conversational French was improved by time spent with French prisoners of war from the Seven-Year's-War in Frenchay, then a small village near Bristol.

She was keen to learn, possessed a sharp intellect and was assiduous in studying and, according to family tradition, began writing at an early age.

In 1758 Jacob established his own girls' boarding school at Trinity Street in Bristol for the elder sisters, Mary and Elizabeth, to run. Hannah became a pupil there when she was 12. Jacob and his wife moved to Stony Hill in the city to open a school for boys.

Hannah became a teacher at her sister's school and it was here that she produced her first literary efforts. These were prompted by trying to find material suitable for her young charges to act in. Her first, written in 1762, was The Search after Happiness (by the mid-1780s some 10,000 copies had been sold).

In 1767 Hannah gave up her share in the school to become engaged to William Turner. After six years, with no wedding in sight, and Turner reluctant to move forward, the engagement was broken off. It was now 1773 and by all accounts Hannah suffered a nervous breakdown and spent some time recuperating in nearby Uphill. Turner then bestowed upon her an annual annuity of £200. This was enough to meet her needs and set her free to pursue a literary career. With that ambition London was her next stop. She travelled there in the winter of 1773/74 together with her sisters, Sarah and Martha.

She had previously written some verses on a production of King Lear staged by the famous actor David Garrick and this led to a lasting friendship with him and a pivotal introduction to the London Literary society. Now she met and charmed Samuel Johnson, Joshua Reynolds and Edmund Burke. Johnson is quoted as saying to her "Madam, before you flatter a man so grossly to his face, you should consider whether or not your flattery is worth having." He would later be quoted as calling her "the finest versifatrix in the English language".

Hannah also became a leading member of the Bluestocking group of women who met to further literary and intellectual pursuits. Here she met women who were to become life-long friends; Elizabeth Montagu, Frances Boscawen, Elizabeth Carter, Elizabeth Vesey and Hester Chapone (Hannah later wrote a celebration of this circle in her 1782 poem The Bas Bleu, or, Conversation, published in 1784).

Her first play, The Inflexible Captive, was staged at Bath in 1775. It was based on the opera, Attilio Regulo, by the Italian Pietro Metastasio (1698-1782) whose works she admired.

Her theatrical career was now in full swing. David Garrick himself produced her next play, Percy, in 1777 as well as writing both the Prologue and Epilogue for it. It was a great success when performed at Covent Garden in December of that year. Her next play, Fatal Falsehood, was staged in 1779, shortly after the death of Garrick. It was less successful but still admired.

With David Garrick now passed (January 20th, 1779) Hannah came to view the theatre as both morally wrong and not where her ambitions now lay. She now began to spend her time advancing her interests in other areas.

In 1781 she first met Horace Walpole, man of letters art historian and Whig politician and now corresponded regularly with him.

A friendship with James Oglethorpe, who had long been concerned with slavery as a moral issue and who was working with Granville Sharp in an early abolitionist capacity, started to awaken Hannah's social conscious.

Hannah turned to religious writing, beginning with her Sacred Dramas in 1782; it rapidly ran through nineteen editions. These and the poems Bas-Bleu and Florio (1786) mark her gradual transition to a more serious and considered view of life and are fully expressed in her Thoughts on the Importance of the Manners of the Great to General Society (1788), and An Estimate of the Religion of the Fashionable World (1790).

In Bristol, in 1784, she discovered the poet Ann Yearsley, the so-called 'poetical milkmaid of Bristol'. With Yearsley destitute, Hannah raised a considerable sum of money for her. Lactilia, as Yearsley was known, published Poems, on Several Occasions in 1785, earning about £600. Hannah and Elizabeth Montagu held the profits in trust to protect them from Yearsley's husband. However Ann wished for the capital to be made over, and made insinuations of stealing against Hannah. The money was released and Hannah felt her reputation had been tarnished.

With the death of Samuel Johnson in December 1784, Hannah moved, with her sister Martha, in 1795, to a cottage at Cowslip Green, near Wrington in rural Somerset, "to escape from the world gradually".

In the summer of 1786, she spent time with Sir Charles and Lady Margaret Middleton at their home in Teston in Kent. Among their guests was the local vicar James Ramsay and a young Thomas Clarkson, both of whom were central to the early abolition campaign against slavery.

In 1787, she met John Newton and the 'Clapham Sect' (a group of wealthy evangelical Christians who lived near Clapham and met at Henry Thornton's house). The group was strongly opposed to the Slave Trade. William Wilberforce was a member of the group and he and Hannah became firm friends.

Hannah contributed much to the running of the newly-founded Abolition Society including, in February 1788, her publication of Slavery, a Poem which has long been recognised as one of the most important poems of the abolition period. The poem dramatically described a mistreated, enslaved female separated from her children and severely questioned Britain's role in the Slave Trade.

Her relationship with members of the society, especially Wilberforce, was close. She spent the summer of 1789 holidaying with Wilberforce in the Peak District, planning for the abolition campaign, which, at the time, was at its height.

Her work now became more evangelical. In the 1790s she wrote several Cheap Repository Tracts which covered moral, religious and political topics and were both for sale or distributed to literate poor people. This coincided with her increasing philanthropic work in the Mendip area.

Beyond any doubt, Hannah was the most influential female member of the Society for Effecting the Abolition of the African Slave Trade.

Hannah wrote many ethical books and tracts: Strictures on the Modern System of Female Education (1799), Hints towards Forming the Character of a Young Princess (1805), Cœlebs in Search of a Wife (only nominally a story, 1809), Practical Piety (1811), Christian Morals (1813), Character of St Paul (1815), Moral Sketches (1819). She was a rapid writer, and her work is consequently discursive, animated and without a rigorous structure.

However the originality and force of Hannah's writings perhaps explains her extraordinary popularity. At the behest of Beilby Porteus, Bishop of London and a leading abolitionist, Hannah wrote many spirited rhymes and prose tales, the earliest of which was Village Politics, by Will Chip (1792), intended to counteract the doctrines of Thomas Paine and the influence of the French Revolution.

The series of Cheap Repository Tracts, eventually led to the formation of the Religious Tracts Society. The Tracts were produced at the rate of three a month between 1795 and 1797.

The most famous is perhaps The Shepherd of Salisbury Plain, describing a family of incredible frugality and contentment. Two million copies of these rapid and telling sketches were circulated, in one year, teaching the poor in rhetoric of the most ingenious homeliness to rely upon the virtues of content, sobriety, humility, industry and reverence for the British Constitution, hatred of the French, trust in God and in the kindness of the gentry.

Several of the Tracts oppose slavery and the slave trade, in particular, the poem The Sorrows of Yamba; or, The Negro Woman's Lamentation, which appeared in November 1795 and which was co-authored with Eaglesfield Smith. However, the tracts have also been noted for their encouragement of social quietism in an age of revolution.

In 1789, she purchased a small house at Cowslip Green in Somerset. Wilberforce encouraged Hannah to set up a Sunday school in Cheddar, where poor children could be taught to read. Soon she and her sisters had set up similar schools throughout the Mendip villages, despite fierce opposition.

She was instrumental in setting up twelve schools by 1800 where reading, the Bible and the catechism were taught to local children. Hannah also donated money to Bishop Philander Chase for the founding of Kenyon College, and a portrait of her hangs there in Peirce Hall.

John Scandrett Harford of Blaise Castle was a prodigious benefactor to More's schools in the 1790s, and Hannah modeled the idealised hero and heroine in Cœlebs in Search of Wife (1809) on Mr and Mrs Harford.

However it cannot be said that Hannah was a staunch supporter of Women's rights. She refused to read Mary Wollstonecraft's Rights of Women, saying "so many women are fond of government... because they are not fit for it. To be unstable and capricious is but too characteristic of our sex". She was also shocked by the movement for female education in France, saying "they run to study philosophy, and neglect their families to be present at lectures in anatomy". She is also said to have turned down an honorary membership of the Royal Society of Literature because she considered her "sex alone a disqualification".

The More sisters also met with a good deal of opposition in their philanthropic works: the farmers thought that education, even to the limited extent of learning to read, would be fatal to agriculture, and the clergy, whose neglect she was making good, accused her of Methodist tendencies.

She continued to oppose slavery throughout her life, but at the time of the Abolition Bill of 1807 (which outlawed the slave trade, but not slavery itself), her health did not permit her to take as active a role in the movement as she had done in the late 1780s, although she maintained a correspondence with Wilberforce and others Abolitionists.

In her later life, she continued to dedicate much of her time to religious writing. Nevertheless, her most popular work was a novel, Cœlebs in Search of a Wife, which appeared in two volumes in 1809 (and which ran to nine editions in 1809 alone).

In 1816, Hannah was still at odds with the French. Following Waterloo she is quoted as saying that 'peace with France is a worse evil than war', and refused to allow a French translation of Cœlebs.

Her last few years were spent at Clifton, people from all parts came to visit her even though her health was fading and she was writing less often.

She lived just long enough to see the act finally abolishing slavery. In July 1833, the Bill to abolish slavery throughout the British Empire passed in the House of Commons, followed by the House of Lords on August 1st.

Hannah More died on September 7th, 1833. She is buried at Church of All Saints, Wrington. In her will she left more than £30,000 to charities and religious societies, the equivalent today of many millions.

www.ingramcontent.com/pod-product-compliance
Lightning Source LLC
Chambersburg PA
CBHW060108050426
42448CB00011B/2651